Humpty Trumpty
Hit a Brick Wall

Humpty Trumpty Hit a Brick Wall

Donald J. Trump's First White House Year in Verse

By David Finkle

Illustrated by Roberta Granzen

PLUM BAY PUBLISHING, LLC

Plum Bay Publishing, LLC
www.clairemckinneypr.com/plumbay

Library of Congress Control Number: 2018936360
ISBN: 978-0-9988617-5-3
Printed in the United States of America

Cover design by Roberta Granzen
Interior layout by Barbara Aronica-Buck
Edited by Sally Fay

For David Edmonds

A Few Opening Words

On January 20, 2017, I needed to relieve my mounting despair over the inauguration as president of a man flabbergastingly unfit for the office. The Mother Goose nursery rhyme line "Humpty Dumpty sat on a wall" came to mind and stuck for obvious reasons: the "wall" part, of course, and the opportunity to recast "Humpty Dumpty" as the rhyming "Humpty Trumpty."

It was a promising way to go forward on whatever I wanted to write. When I finished that first multi-stanza effort, I'd had such a good time that I decided it might be fun to do more—maybe even come up with one quatrain or so a day for the new president's first year in office.

It also occurred to me that making up a poem for each of 365 days—and one extra on the first anniversary of the fateful inauguration—was a big challenge. I wondered if there would be material enough to fill a year and a day.

Why not try it anyway? I forged ahead, and in only a few short weeks I noticed that sufficient material was hardly a concern. There was much more than enough, and it looked as if things were extremely unlikely to change.

So I kept going, realizing as the months passed that I was accumulating a verse chronicle of what Elizabeth II—were she keeping a close eye on American politics—might have called an *annus horribilis*.

When 366 days were over and I had not missed a single one, I had compiled this book, in which many of the verses don't rise above doggerel. Then again, does Donald J. Trump deserve anything more than doggerel? As the old saying goes: Read it and weep.

Humpty Trumpty
Hit a Brick Wall

January 2017

January 20

Humpty Trumpty talked of a wall.
Humpty Trumpty built none at all.
Mike Pence's sources and Mike Pence's men
Couldn't put Trumpty together again.

Humpty Trumpty calls Putin pet,
Humpty Trumpty, marionette.
Tillerson's sources and Tillerson's men
Couldn't put Trumpty together again.

Humpty Trumpty calls up friend Jeff.
Humpty Trumpty is so tone-deaf.
Priebus's sources and Priebus's men
Couldn't put Trumpty together again.

Humpty Trumpty took on the press.
Humpty Trumpty had no success.
Sean Spicer's sources and Sean Spicer's men
Couldn't put Trumpty together again.

Humpty Trumpty talked immigrants.
Judges all have laughed at him since.
Steve Bannon's sources and Steve Bannon's men
Couldn't put Trumpty together again.

Humpty Trumpty mocked climate change.
Humpty Trumpty showed his short range.
Ryan Zinke's sources and Ryan Zinke's men
Couldn't put Trumpty together again.

Humpty Trumpty spoke with Taiwan.
Humpty Trumpty blabbed on and on.
Kellyanne's sources and Kellyanne's men
Couldn't put Trumpty together again.

Humpty Trumpty picked out DeVos.
Humpty Trumpty favors the dross.
All Jared's sources and all Jared's men
Couldn't put Trumpty together again.

Humpty Trumpty tweets quite a lot.
Humpty Trumpty misses the plot.
Ivanka's sources and Ivanka's men
Couldn't put Trumpty together again.

January 21
The only one who acts
On alternative facts
Is he who chose to rise
By telling all those lies.

January 22
Hey there, Sean Spicer,
Perhaps you'd be nicer
If you weren't controlled
To repeat lies you're told.

January 23
All of us are in suspense
In re: our new veep, Mike Pence,
So I'll ask, to end this verse,
"Prezzie's bad, but is Pence worse?"

January 24
Our new prez is giving orders
In regards to southern borders,
Surely now, he should plan a de-
Tailed plot to wall off Canada.

January 25
Orwell's *1984*
Is atop the charts once more.
It's a book the prez might need,
If, that is, he still can read.

January 26
Our new prez has put a freeze
On a lot of refugees.
Now if he could sign some laws
Banning all his mental flaws.

January 27
Steven Bannon, what a man!
Look, his surname starts with "ban."
Look, he has our new prez Trump
Planting kisses on his rump.

January 28
Steven Bannon of the White House—
More and more a great, big fright house:
Would you say it's no red herring
That the guy is Donald's Goering?

January 29

Throughout his months out on the stump,
Trump ticked off the things he'd trump.
He named crisis after crisis,
But where is that plan for Isis?

January 30

If the new prez eases through
Right-wing Neil Gorsuch,
You know just what next he'll do:
Plug away for more such.

January 31

Trump plays the tough taskmaster.
He watches ev'ry rating.
He terms things "a disaster."
He likes taskmaster baiting.

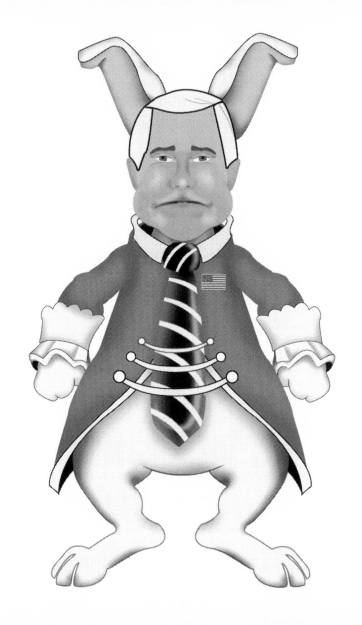

February 2017

February 1
"Let's get rid of Dodd-Frank.
It's been a disaster.
That way ev'ry odd bank
Can trick people faster."

February 2
Trump terms the judge "a so-called judge."
Yup, that's sure what he sez.
Hey, that gives all of us a nudge
To dub him "so-called prez."

February 3
Take the case of Ms. DeVos,
Facing a potential loss:
For charter schools she often cares,
But not so much for grizzly bears.

February 4
You know it's sure as shootin'
The so-called prez loves Putin.
He said at his first glance,
"At last my true bromance."

February 5
I've just learned the women's march—
During which I flexed an arch—
Was paid. So I say, "What the heck!
Why haven't I received my check?"

February 6
Our so-called prez dislikes the press.
He points out their dishonest stress.
Is he dishonest? No, forsooth.
He just has no regard for truth.

February 7
The so-called prez has lost in court,
But has he deigned to be a sport?
No, he is angry in ALL CAPS—
Another step towards his collapse.

February 8
Cagey Michael Flynn,
Wanting Don to win,
Reached out quick to Vlad.
Will he say, "My bad"?

February 9
Donald values Kellyanne,
Spinning ev'ry way she can.
Now she's shilling for Ivanka,
Who owes her a great big "Thank ya."

February 10
The so-called prez says voter fraud
Is very, very, very broad.
Of course, what he insists is true.
I voted twice. Well, didn't you?

February 11
You know the saying, "In like Flynn."
Today there's the reverse.
Now "Out like Flynn" is happenin'.
It makes a great new curse.

February 12

Hello, operator, put me through to Vlad.
Thanks, my friend, for making Hillary look bad.
Keep in touch, my dear friend, with my top-most aides
They will sign off daily on all Ukraine raids.

February 13

A wall he said he'd build.
Constituents were thrilled.
Construction has begun—
The walled-up White House one.

February 14

Our new leader faced the press,
Proving he's a total mess.
All he did was boast and whinge,
Making the whole planet cringe.

February 15

Donald Trump is at a rally,
Ready to fudge on the tally.
He will spout the same old lies
That no single smart soul buys.

February 16
Croaking like a boastful frog
In the role of demagogue,
Trump addressed constituents
With the same tired arguments.

February 17
Now Trump's goin' off on Sweden.
What reports has he been readin'?
Hand me no ifs, ands or buts.
This poor guy's completely nuts.

February 18
So what's it like for Michael Pence,
Who's seen a lot of presidents
And ends up serving this crackpot?
It's not the winningest jackpot.

February 19
Let's hope the Trumpkin isn't keen
On having dinner with the Queen,
Since all the eager voting Brits
Would like his invite torn to bits—
Plus one assumes the long-run Queen
Herself considers him obscene.

February 20
Ev'ry week he's playing golf,
At his Mar-a-Lago,
Ripping all us tax dupes off.
What a slick farrago!

February 21
So-called prez is on a bender
Undermining all cross-gender,
Bowing to Conservatives
Who hate how the Other lives.

February 22
Have you seen democracy
Turn into demo-crazy
Now that Trump, our so-called prez,
Fills the presidential chaise?

February 23
Donald Trump, the narrow winner,
Won't attend the press corps dinner—
No Chris Rock, no Amy Schumer,
Since he has no sense of humor.

February 24

Meryl Streep is overrated.
Hamilton is overrated.
So the so-called prez has stated.
You diss him. You're overrated.
Jimmy Kimmel? Overrated.
Guess who's *really* overrated?
Guess whose ego is inflated?
Guess who thinks he's celebrated—
Acts as if he's consecrated?
Trump, whose head is carbonated.

February 25

Who's the saddest man you know?
"So sad, so sad," he will go.
Failing "Times"—so sad, so sad.
"SNL"—so sad, so sad.
"So sad" is his frequent song,
Even though he's always wrong.
Too damn bad he's so, so sad.
Kinda makes me very glad.

February 26

Do you hear the thund'rous clash?
That's the sound of Donald's fasc-
Istic rumblings you have heard.
Now if you'd please pass the word.

February 27

How about that scamp Jeff Sessions'
Tight-lipped Russia talks confessions?
'Publicans will all deny it.
Democrats will never buy it.

February 28

"Who can I blame today?
Who can I name today?
Who can I shame today?
Let's see who mocked me.
Who can I slam today?
Who can I scam today?
Who can I damn today?
Let's see who knocked me.
Who can I blast today—
Hoist up the mast today
And call dumb-assed today?
Let's see who dissed me.
Who can I cuss today,
Bother and fuss today,
Under-the-bus today?
Let's see who hissed me.
There must be someone here.
There must be someone near,
Someone for my weak leer,
Someone to fill with fear.
Someone to cause great sorrow.
Then who to kick tomorrow?"

March 2017

March 1

Oh, that rascal Prez Obama,
Giving Donald such great drama,
Wire-tapping tall Trump Tower,
Hour after sneaky hour.
Betcha Michelle wasn't missin'
Having herself quite a listen,
As were Sasha and Malia.
What a horrible idea.

March 2

(partly to the tune of Georgia Gibbs's "Tweedlee Dee")
Tweetlee Tweetlee Tweetlee Dee!
I am on a tweeting spree.
First I'll take Obama down,
Then get Arnold, that sad clown.
Tweetlee Tweetlee Tweetlee Dee!
Tweetlee Tweetlee Tweetlee Dum!
What a tweeter I've become.
Vladdie Putin—I'll call prince

And make CIA guys wince.
Tweetlee Tweetlee Tweetlee Dum!
Tweetlee Tweetlee Tweetlee Dow!
I'll keep tweeting here and now.
Can't you see I really aim
T'make the Constitution lame?
Tweetlee Tweetlee Tweetlee Dow!
Tweetlee Tweetlee Tweetlee Dot!
I'll give tweeting all I've got.
People say that I am seething.
Not at all—I'm merely teething.
Tweetlee Tweetlee Tweetlee Dot!

March 3

Yoo-hoo, yoo-hoo, Kellyanne,
Are you now an also-ran?
Is this an unhappy ending—
No more out there Trump defending,
No more out there Trump explaining?
Understand, I'm not complaining.

March 4

So far is he presidential,
Which you'd think is quite essential?
Still it's hardly evidential.
Any sign's coincidental.

March 5

Here's a trick we all should try:
Come right out and tweet a lie,
Then tell Congress, "Turn up heat!"
While we frame our next fake tweet.

March 6

"Who else saw it's complicated?"
Ev'rybody else, it's stated.
Now you are behind a health plan
Best described as Trump's new stealth plan.

March 7

Here I sit at four a.m.,
Tweeting against all of them.
Anyone who's mocked my name
I'll embarrass and defame.
So what if I have to lie?
That's just me, a clever guy,
Much the smartest guy I know,
Outsmarting all of you below.

March 8

Yoo-hoo, yoo-hoo, Scottie Pruitt,
We all knew that you would do it.
(That includes Vlad Putin's chump,
Better known as Donald Trump.)
As the EPA you man it,
We knew you'd condemn our planet
Global warming, you'd deny it
Just as quick as you could cry it.

March 9

Holy moly man oh man!
So-called prezzie's new health plan!
Holy moly man alive!
Older folks may not survive.
Holy moly love a duck!
If you're poor, you're out o' luck.
Holy moly what the hell!
If you're rich, you'll do quite well.
Holy moly holy spit!
Now what do you think of it?

March 10

Tillerson—the one called Rex—
Doesn't' want reporters' checks.
Tillerson—the sec. of state—
Exits when they congregate.
They may press him for a while.
He'll just look at them and smile.
What's he hiding with the smirk—
That he doesn't do much work?

March 11

Kellyanne tells all she can
Of Barack's wire-tapping plan.
Microwaves, she says it's true,
Could be listening in on you.
Ev'ry blender might be set
To record each tete-a-tete.
Watch your toaster and your clock
Just in case it's taking stock.
Folks, if you avert the scan,
Send your thanks to Kellyanne.

March 12

You can bet that blame-free Trump—
When the health plan hits its slump,
And you know damn well it will—
He'll insist it's not his bill.

March 13

For sure, you know about Rasputin.
Whose name includes the news name Putin.
The first one had an empress cling.
The next has Trumpnik on a string.

March 14

Trump's new budget has cruel parts.
He completely cuts the arts,
Blocks the so dishonest media
Saying, "Just check Wikipedia."

March 15

No handshake for leader Merkel—
One more time our White House jerk'll
Grab the chance to demonstrate
He has the mental age of eight.

March 16

A man who cancels Meals on Wheels
Is surely not a man who feels.
A man who tells kids "No free lunch"
Is definitely out to lunch.
At least that's gotta be the hunch
On how he acts to face the crunch.

March 17

Will so-called prez apologize
Or even just acknowledgize
His baseless tweets? Of course, he won't.
Look, men who have no morals don't.

March 18

The so-called prez, that world-class clown,
Sends out a tweet, then doubles down.
We all will wait a lifetime long
For him to say the words "I'm wrong."

March 19

Wanna know how low he gets?
He talks big and issues threats.
When he lacks the health care vote,
Let's all duck the Trumpnik's quotes.

March 20

Ivanka has her White House room
From which she expects to loom.
Doing what? I'll put you wise.
Her sole purpose is: She spies.

March 21

Yoo-hoo, yoo-hoo, Paul D. Ryan,
Of your health bill: Few are buyin'.
You may think that you're a bruiser,
But the prez thinks you're a loser.

March 22

So-called prez said from Day 1
'bama care would be long gone.
Looks like that's now been undone.
So let's build a wall, my son.

March 23

All the health care's gross inaction
Also served as big distraction
From the prez's many failings,
Many which could end in jailings.

March 24

Ivanka did some fancy graspin'
Taking Jared out to Aspen,
For some ultra-fancy playin',
And, of course, you know who's payin'.

March 25

Donald Trump is no brain trust.
Let's all face it, since we must.
About those two grown boys of his,
Neither is a mental whiz.
Of required vision stuff,
What they have's not near enough.

March 26

Devin Nunes sneaks around,
Hiding ev'rything he's found.
You might think there'd be recusal.
But you're gonna get refusal.

March 27

Yoo-hoo, hey, Paul Manafort,
Won't you kindly tell us more?
Have you heard from Russia lately?
We would like your answer greatly.

March 28

Michael Flynn demands immunity
So he'll speak out with impunity,
Which could mean that very soon a "T"—
Stands for "Treason"—we'll all swoon ta see.

March 29

Michael Ellis, Ezra Cohen-Watnick—
More names for the fat Russia plotnik.
Just how many will be clocked up
Till the motley crew is locked up?

March 30

Ivanka wants to be a daughter,
Which is really what she oughter,
But her truly preferred story
Is that fashion inventory.
Seven hundred forty mill
Our princess boasts on Cap'tol Hill.

March 31

"Hillary, apologize,"
Our so-called prezzie tweets,
As if for all his monstrous lies
Of humble pie he eats.

April 2017

April 1

Autocrat, kleptocrat—
So-called prez is fine with that,
'Cause, of course, you know it's true:
He'd enjoy those titles, too.

April 2

What about his plan for Isis?
Just another postponed crisis?
What's he doing in re Syria
Of his other mad deliria?

April 3

Whatever happened to Kellyanne Conway?
Can it be true that she really has gone 'way?
What of the future for Breitbart's Steve Bannon?
Is he about to be shot from a cannon?

April 4

Trump's shot out many a missile.
How much does it indicate this'll
Become a wide split with Vlad Putin
Or just a brief trending like gluten?

April 5

Mitch McConnell sure did muster
Votes to kill the filibuster.
Now Supreme Court future will be
Democrats v. The GOP.

April 6

Jared here, Jared there,
Jared Kushner ev'rywhere,
Verifying that old saw:
"It helps to be a son-in-law."

April 7

Foreign policy under Trump
Looks to be in quite a slump.
Those who speak and whom we see
One by one, they disagree.

April 8

How about that Bill O'Reilly
Chasing all those women slyly,
While the prez sings his old song,
"My friend Bill did nothing wrong."

April 9

Yoo-hoo, yoo-hoo, Eric Trump!
How come you are such a lump?
What on earth will you become
When ev'rything you say is dumb?

April 10

How long can it be till Sean
Spicer is completely gone?
After all, his many gaffes
Are no longer good for laughs.

April 11

Do you think Trump's acting normal?
Do you think his standard form'll
Alter with an on-job shake-up?
If you do, you need to wake up.

April 12

Has he tried to pivot?
How long do you give it?
Will he hope to live it
Or just negative it?

April 13

Let's just say that Kim Jong-un,
Who's a very grim young'n,
Has his little kiddy match
In so-called prez. That's Donnie, natch.

April 14

Don't you get the least bit queasy
When the so-called prez says "easy"?
We all know he's in the throes
Of how little stuff he knows.

April 15

What's all this about his audit?
We all know that it's a fraud. It
Is his way of not confiding
All the dirt he thinks he's hiding.

April 16

Calling Erdogan in Turkey,
Our new prez was being jerk-y.
So was getting downright kiss-y
With Abdel Fattah el-Sisi.

April 17

He'll only use superlatives.
That's the realm in which he lives.
If he has some chocolate cake,
It's the best the world can bake.
So to use his big-word thirst:
As a prez, he's much the worst.

April 18

Daily, this is how he gets—
Hot to issue hollow threats.
Seems it's all he wants to do.
Soon he'll likely threaten you.

April 19

100 days, 100 days—
Ain'tcha fed up with the phrase?
As they dwindle down to none,
We know nothing will get done.

April 20

Twitter, twitter, twitter, twitter—
Donald Trump's a heavy hitter.
When he's feeling crossed and bitter,
He dispenses all that litter.
Twitter, twitter, twitter, twitter
Goes that clearly nutty critter,
Causing all of us to titter,
"He just needs a baby-sitter."
Add this to the Trump con list:
Making cash hand over fist,
Like that big DC hotel.
Tax returns? So far, no tell.

April 21

Prezzie takes a tax-cut swerve—
Spinning on the Laffer curve—
Which could hike the deficit,
But he is downplaying it.

April 22

When he was out on the stump,
Exec Orders he would dump.
Now he has that White House pen,
Those EOs are in again.

April 23

He just loves his tax reform,
And you, you mustn't mock it,
'Cause that gosh-darn tax reform
Puts money in his pocket.

April 24

So he's had his hundred days,
Which he now deems just a phase.
Do you really think that he
Could effect a winning spree?
You'd be dazed if you say "Yup."
Were he smart, he'd just give up,
But, of course, he isn't smart.
When he deals he has no art.

April 25

He's played a game of three-card monte
That may fool your dear old auntie.
Don't you think, you other guys,
That it's come time you all got wise?

April 26

Dictators he likes to defend.
If you're a tyrant, you're his friend.
The reason here is sad but true.
He'd like to be a tyrant, too.

April 27

He's honored to meet Kim Jong-un
Or Duterte, another one.
He seems to get a special thrill
From heads of state who like to kill.

April 28

"I stand by nothing," he's just said.
For once he's told the truth.
Otherwise, what's in his head
Is pretty much uncouth.

April 29

GOP so hot to still
Prez Obama's health care bill—
To replace it with who-knows,
Long as that ACA goes.

April 30

"How'm I doon? Am I doon okay?"—
Said in the White House garden.
Now that he's had his vict'ry day,
He'll watch resistance harden.

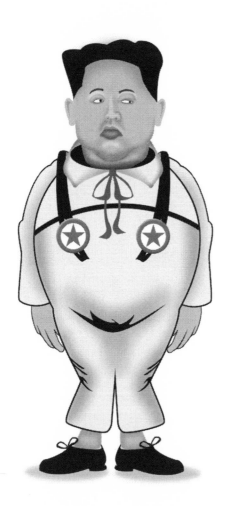

May 2017

May 1

"Believe me," he has often said.
Of course, we don't believe him.
We know what we should do instead:
Regard his truths as waaay slim.

May 2

All us good ol' white boys in the frat
Scotched the ACA bill just like that,
Then we hit the White House to cheer there
And to show 'em how much we don't care.

May 3

Surely, he's no big brain whiz.
Ignorant is what he is.
Just how backward can he be?
Have him speak on history.

May 4

"You shouldn't trust this Sally Yates,"
The so-called prez supremely states.
You wonder at how low he'll stoop?
If you believe him, you're the dupe.

May 5

"Those of you who know me
Know I do my best,
Like getting rid of Comey
And soon all the rest."

May 6

Who's the planet's biggest yes-man?
I'm not gonna make you guess, man.
I won't keep you in suspense—
That butt-kisser's Michael Pence.

May 7

He commands 'em to be loyal
Since he thinks he's kinda royal.
If loyal is not what he gets,
Then he starts to fire off threats.

May 8
Who's he gonna nominate?
Someone he will say is "great,"
Someone he'll choose on a whim,
Someone who'll be loyal to him.

May 9
While the Trump brat does truth vi'lence,
Mitch McConnell keeps his silence.
Ditto all his caucus schmoozers—
Yes, the GOP, those losers.

May 10
You've laughed at his funny lips.
Now you know they're good for slips.
Now because he loves to brag,
One cat's way out of a bag.
Now because he's immature,
The US is less secure.

May 11
Here's the burden of Trump's song:
"I never, ever do things wrong."
In your turn, you're s'posed to chime,
"I'm sure you're right time after time."

May 12

Subject of a mad witch hunt—
This is not what he would want.
So when he's not out to letch,
That's when he will kvetch and kvetch.

May 13

And now Trump's off to foreign lands
With not one brief he understands.
Instead, he'll make a ton of gaffes,
And when he makes them, no one laughs.

May 14

Now that Donnie's said his howdys
To the gang of leading Saudis,
Are we kinda thinking he
Is now convinced he's royalty?

May 15

Donald Trump, so hard to teach,
Donald Trump, so hard to reach,
Gave at last a slip-free speech,
Gave a talk without a breach.
Still, he's no day at the beach.

May 16

Comey is a true nutcase.
That's what the prez asserts,
But the hand-to-God nutcase
Is he who makes those blurts.

May 17

"I never mentioned Israel," he said
Without his face becoming flushed and red.
This, to Israel's Netanyahu, Bibi
Gets you asking just how dumb can he be.

May 18

   ACT I
He: (on exiting the jet) I want to hold your hand.
She: (pushing his hand away) I don't want to hold your hand.
   ACT II
He: (on exiting the jet a few days later) I want to hold your
   hand.
She: (pushing his hand away) I don't have time to hold your
   hand. I need to get my windswept hair out of my face.

May 19
Russian Intelligence (softly, with big stick):
First, Michael Flynn
Will get us in,
Then more support
From Manafort.

May 20
Now Jared's in the spotlight,
And it's a very hot light.
They say he's under "scrutiny."
Let's all assume it's Putin-y.

May 21
So-called prez just went abroad
To confirm he's quite a fraud.
He chastised his peers in NATO
Through a speech far short of Plato.

May 22
Back from his trip,
Resuming tweets,
He's lost his grip:
"Fake news" repeats.

May 23

They talk about "reset."
They talk about "pivot."
Too bad he can't be set
To honestly live it.

May 24

What's he done
Since Day 1?
Immigrants?
Little since.
Tax reform?
Hardly warm.
Build the wall?
Not at all.
Things abroad?
Underawed.
Lots of stress,
No success.

May 25

What that White House jerk'll
Say on leader Merkel
Likely is more hector.
He's our global spectre.

May 26

Don't you think this time it
'S best to face the climate
And the way it's changing?
'Stead, Trump is deranging.

May 27

Paris accord: Withdrawn.
Steve Bannon strong-arms on.
Rest of the world is Trumped.
Prez Trump, too, should be dumped.

May 28

What rhymes with covfefe?
Commander-in-chief?
Commander-in-chef?
Or is Trump just tone-, er, type-deaf?

May 29

By now everyone agrees
On Trump's foot-in-mouth disease.
There simply is no debate
On his gift to alienate.

May 30

How about our in-law Jared
And his morals: Plainly arid.
Same goes for our rich Ivanka:
Ethics-less there, too—and thank ya.
Now here comes the explanation.
These cute kids have dispensation.

May 31

He ran
On travel ban,
Began
A travel ban,
His plan:
A travel ban.
He ran
A travel ban.
Broad span,
This travel ban.
To Ann:
It is a ban.

To Dan:
It's not a ban.
To Fran:
It is a ban.
To Jan:
It's not a ban.
To Nan:
It is a ban.
To Stan:
It's not a ban.
To Xian:
It is a ban.
Hey, man,
Go get a tan.

June 2017

June 1

James B. Comey,
Show me, show me,
And show Trump
Who says, "You owe me!"
Tell him, "Prez,
You're way below me.
There's no way
That you can throw me."

June 2

Don called Jim "nutcase."
He called him "showboat."
Now tell me what case
Deserves a "No" vote?

June 3

Trump shouts out he's vindicated.
Forget it, pal, you're indicated.
With the skinny Mueller musters,
You'll be outta here gangbusters.

June 4

And so is Trump taping
With no one escaping?
You know that he doesn't.
Taping Comey? He wasn't.
And if he was somehow,
Those tapes are long gone now.

June 5

At Sessions' sessions
True confessions
Were transgressions.

June 6

Here's the latest White House color:
Donald Trump may fire Bob Mueller,
Leaving us all realizing
Such a turn is not surprising.

June 7

Let's give praise to Donald Trump.
Let's plant kisses on his rump.
Let's be like his cabinet,
Bow as low as we can get.
Let's be good Republicans
And kowtow to his worst plans.

June 8

When hiking the campaign trail,
Donald Trump would rail and rail,
Violence a frequent shout.
Now he thinks he'll weasel out.

June 9

He doesn't see that each new tweet
Is drawing him near to defeat.
No matter what, he hasn't ceased.
The opposite: He's just increased.
All the tweets on which he's binged
Confirm the fact that he's unhinged.

June 10

Who would want to be his lawyer
And have him as an employer?
Who would want to do his bidding?
I would want to. No, I'm kidding.
Who would want to tend those mad fits?
Mr. Dowd and Mr. Kasowitz.

June 11

Imagine you're a White House aide
Attempting daily to be heard
By someone who likes to degrade
And so can't hear a single word.
Imagine that you've stayed and stayed,
Does not your self-esteem get blurred?

June 12

Is he is, or is he ain't in question?
Is he on the spot, or is he not?
He confirmed he was to the suggestion,
But his lawyer says that's not the plot.

June 13

Has he read his new health bill?
Like as not he never will.
He could care just what it says
If it passes. That's our prez.

June 14

Are you sick and tired of him?
Are you fed up to the brim,
Steamed at all his flam and flim,
Keen to tear him limb from limb?
Why not go and take a swim,
Join a choir or else a gym?
That's the way to treat it, Slim.
Otherwise, it's all too grim.

June 15

Don't be quick to cross off,
Don't make haste to toss off
That young Dem, Jon Ossoff.
Best scratch the White House boss off.

June 16

Because the UK people begged
The Brit invite has been reneged.
The White House bows to those requests.
This way the prez avoids protests.

June 17

Donald Trump has an idea.
He's announced that he can see a
Solar panel at the border.
Just another wishful order.

June 18

Seems a shame that Johnny Depp
Has again defamed his rep,
Said some things of prezzie Trump,
Making him a worser chump.

June 19

Mitch McConnell's
Health plan con'll
Do us all in:
A mortal sin.

June 20

Victories he claims forever.
Are they real? Hardly ever.
There's Judge Gorsuch. Yes, that's one.
After him, the list is done.

June 21

Trump is so chock-full of fear
He lets nearly no one near.
Elder daughter shares the joy—
Clearly not his youngest boy.

June 22

Would you like to guess at who's
Been promoting his fake news?
Who has put his face so plump
On a false Time cover? Trump!

June 23

Trump decided he would shriek a
Nasty slur at hostess Mika.
Then he thought he'd stretch his show
And tweet foul words on bridegroom Joe.
This is how he leads the globe.
Time to start a mental probe.

June 24

If you're traveling abroad,
All you hear is, "He's a fraud,"
And you can't put up a fight,
'Cause they're all completely right.

June 25

In France they now have E. Macron.
Compare him with our own man Don.
The first is young, intelligent.
The other's our thug president.

June 26

The prez is off the rails again,
Once more attacking CNN.
This time he tweets a video.
In French, "Trump" rhymes with "idiot."

June 27

Prez Trump thinks mock wrestling
Is for him the bes' li'l thing,
But the sport's a metaphor
For a faker we deplore.

June 28

Donald Trump will fly away
France-ward for Bastille Day.
Place no bets our graceless prez
Will join for the "La Marseillaise."
He'll just try to look his best
While the French crowds all protest.

June 29

Off to Poland Donald jets,
Raving on of dire threats,
But leaves out, throughout his frets,
He's as dire as it gets.

June 30

Trump keeps plugging US first,
While he heads for US worst.
Merkel, Macron *et al* thrust,
Leaving Donald in the dust.

July 2017

July 1

Donald made no stern request—
Russian hacking wasn't pressed.
When Vlad put him to the test,
He swiped Trump like any pest.
That's how Putin came out best.
Now we all await the rest.

July 2

Wouldn't we all like a look
At an even single book
Owned by prezzie Donald Trump?
Wanna bet the odds aren't plump?

July 3

Donald's sons
Are the ones
To begin
His do-in.

July 4

Wassup? Wassup? Wassup?
Trump's troops have lawyered up.
So many have been signed
There're no more you can find.

July 5

Donald Trump can't brush a-
Side his links with Russia,
And his son, Don Junior
Than his dad is loonier.

July 6

Are you asking which hunt?
Trump calls it the witch-hunt.
It's that known-as-sich hunt.
He'd prefer a ditch-hunt.

July 7

Early, Jared Kushner saw
That his famous dad-in-law
Played an active lying game,
So he said, "I'll do the same."
And that's how the clever youth
Jettisoned the honest truth.
Donald Jr. said just four.
Oops, no, there were really more.
It could be five. It could be six—
Or maybe more into the mix.
Perhaps it's eight. Perhaps it's twenty.
No matter what, it sure is plenty.

July 8

'Vanka, Jared out in Aspen,
Graspin', graspin', graspin', graspin',
Makin' money by the cart,
Thinkin' they look very smart.
Here's the lowdown on their looks:
They look like a pair of crooks.

July 9

Trump said Madame Macron looks "fit,"
But what are we to make of it?
He meant it as a compliment,
Our foolish, oaf-ish president,
But it's a sexist, sad remark
That proves he's still so in the dark.
And it's completely ageist, too.
A man like that to lead won't do.

July 10

Trump bigly talks of signing bills,
As if to give us lots of thrills.
So now let's take a little pause,
Then have him list his brand-new laws.

July 11

Trump informed us that Day 1
Repeal/Replace would quick be done.
Six months on he lacks true gains,
As Obamacare remains.

July 12

Six months go by so darn fast.
What has Trump done that'll last?
Lots of damage globally,
Zilch-squat-nada noble-ly.
What's the end to this sad tale?
Looks like someone's doomed to fail.

July 13

Sessions felt he must recuse—
Not what Donald Trump would choose.
So the prez said, "I'll abuse."
Guess what? This is not fake news.

July 14

To Sean Spicer say bye-bye.
He has told his final lie
In defense of Donald Trump,
Now he's tossed out on his rump.

July 15

Scaramucci, known as "Mooch,"
Now is prezzie Trump's new pooch,
But should he just once offend,
It's the doghouse as his end.

July 16

(to the tune of "I Never Promised You a Rose Garden"):
In the Rose Garden.
I'd like to promise me a full pardon—
Have it extended
To everyone I've befriended.

July 17

After Jared's testimony,
His short statement sounded phony.
Although he presents as tone-y,
What he says is pure baloney.

July 18

Loyalty is where he lives—
The White House resident.
He takes, of course, but never gives,
And that's our president.

July 19

"You're fired!" is his fav'rite pitch.
It seems more like a constant twitch
That explains his cruel aggressions
'Gainst his AG, poor Jeff Sessions.

July 20

Donald Trump and Tony Mooch—
Separated twins at birth.
Ain't it fun to watch them smooch?
Ain't it worth a girth of mirth?

July 21

He's a man with a plan.
He's a man with a ban,
And he'll ban when he can.
He'd ban Afghanistan.

July 22

Two four six eight!
Whom can Trump humiliate?
Eight six four two!
Anyone nearby will do.
Three five seven nine!
Tony Mooch will fall in line.
Nine seven five three!
And he's vulgar as can be.

July 23

Donald Trump will never speak
On the horrors of last week
Or the present White House curse:
What is bad will just get worse.

July 24

He had ten full days to rule—
Prove himself the perfect fool.
So goodbye to Tony Mooch,
Kelly now has told him, "Scooch."

July 25

Here's a quote from Donald Trump:
"The White House is a real dump."
Yes, it's true, we must declare.
It's a dump when you're dumped there.

July 26

Donald Trump has signed that bill,
Though it was against his will.
Then he sent a peevish tweet
Hinting he will not retreat.

July 27

Though he may not ken it,
He has lost the Senate.
And the House reps also
Plan to make him crawl slow.

July 28

Mueller has his new grand jury,
Which has put Trump in a fury.
Is a Mueller firing closer?
At this point it looks like "No, sir!"

July 29

Donald Trump is at Bedminster
Where he can be very sins'ter,
Where he can be very bitter,
Where he'll twitter, twitter, twitter.

July 30

Here's some news that's slightly stunning:
New York Times says Pence is running,
Which means Trump in his known way'll
See this as a yuge betrayal.

July 31

Here's the clever advert heading
For your cool Bedminster wedding:
"With your economic top buy
You receive a Prez Trump drop-by."
While you're knotting to your honey,
Why should prez not make some money?

August 2017

August 1
Donald Trump and Kim Jong-un,
With their you-will-pay pens,
Are so much like grim young'n-
S fighting in their playpens.

August 2
Knock, knock, knock. "Paul Manafort,
Where's your hot stuff? Where'dya store't?
We're the searching FBI.
Trump can't stop us. Let him try."

August 3
Donald Trump said "fire and fury."
All of us became his jury.
We said, "He's the White House clown."
What does he do? Doubles down.
He says that's not "tough enough."
What if someone calls his bluff?

August 4

Trump is bashing Mitch McConnell,
Just the kind of thing that Don'll
Do when he won't take the blame:
Sully someone else's name.

August 5

In the White House, there exists
Several white supremacists.
Trumpnik must admire them.
Otherwise, he'd fire them.

August 6

Charlottesville, oh Charlottesville,
Emblem of a nation's ill—
With a coward president
As the White House resident.
If you want to start a list,
He's our lead supremacist.

August 7

Donald Trump is such a jerk—
Got back quick to Frazier (Merck).
What about the White House folks
Who make up some office spokes—
Bannon, Gorka, Miller (Steve)?
How soon do you think they'll leave?
Never, we can all be sure.
In Trump's White House, they're secure.

August 8

Has Donald Trump, that plump ass,
Just lost his moral compass?
No, that's not what he's done.
He never really had one.

August 9

Of people who inspire,
We now have Heather Heyer.
Of those who make us grow,
Her mother, Susan Bro.
Of people we must dump,
We all have Donald Trump.

August 10
(to the tune of Joni Mitchell's "Both Sides Now")
I've looked at Donald's "both sides" now,
From left and right, and still somehow
I only see a snake-like crawl.
I really can't take Trump at all.
I've looked at Donald's "both sides" now,
From in and out, and still somehow
I only see he craves a brawl.
I really can't bear Trump at all.
I've looked at Donald's "both sides" now
From high and low, and still somehow
I only see a devil's fall.
I really can't stand Trump at all.

August 11
So Bannon is now out,
But don't have any doubt
That Trump needs no assist
As chief supremacist.

August 12

Don't you think it's very strange
That people think he still might change?
Good grief, the guy is 71.
The years when he could change are gone.

August 13

Straight to God's ear from your lips
Let's all hope that this eclipse
Is the first of two this year
And that Trump's is drawing near.

August 14

Donald Trump once had a plan:
Get out of Afghanistan.
Now he has a brand-new plan:
Let's stay in Afghanistan.
What a man, oh, what a man!
Aren't we grateful that he ran?

August 15

Donald went to Phoenix,
And just what did he fix
At his ugly rally?
Zero is the tally.

August 16

Yes, Trump is very famous,
But he's an ignoramus,
And though he's also wealthy,
He's mentally unhealthy.

August 17

Donald boasts he has "two tones"
As if that were a plus.
Sounds of worldwide angry groans
Come from the rest of us.

August 18

Is the president unfit?
You can bet the farm on it.
A man who pardons Sheriff Joe
Best hail a shrink, get set and go.

August 19

Trump thinks he's above the law.
He mocks the Constitution.
The guy is one huge human flaw
For which there's no solution.

August 20
There is no equivocation.
Trump prefers a racist nation.
From Maine to Texas to Ohio
He backs folks like Joe Arpaio.

August 21
Donald Trump, that business man,
Thinks that as his business ran
He can run the country, too,
But, good grief, that's just not true.

August 22
News of Russia drip-drip-drips
Prompting Trump to purse his lips
And try yet another lie
That his base will gladly buy.

August 23
Donald went to Texas
And the Harvey nexus
To say he was proud
Of the turnout crowd.

August 24

Here is how our Flotus feels:
She does best when wearing heels.
They are proper anytime—
From a ball to Harvey slime.

August 25

Is there a way to block a
Plan to scuttle DACA?
Is there some way to bump
That spiteful Donald Trump?

August 26

Of course, the plan is no tell
About Trump's Moscow hotel.
Best to check the loot in-
Volving wise guy Putin.

August 27

Donald Trump is so uncouth
When he disregards the truth.
We now know he just was sour
Claiming Barack tapped his Tower.

August 28
Sessions in his numbskull fashion
Kept on talking of "compassion."
Whose compassion, pray, this is?
Surely, not the Trump's or his.

August 29
Ignorance is what Trump chooses.
Why care that the planet loses?
He still nixes climate change
As Irma blows in Flor'da range.

August 30
Ev'ry time the prezzie speaks,
Saying something like "two weeks,"
You can bet that that endeavor
Will occur the twelfth of never.

August 31
Is Trump really one of them?
Is he once again a Dem?
If you think that, you'd be wrong
He is never much for long.

September 2017

September 1
How about that slick Scott Pruitt?
Climate change? He's not into it.
Harvey? Irma? Sleeps right through it.
When he wakes, he just says, "Screw it!"

September 2
Irma may not be too sweet,
But she's silenced Donald's tweet.
Irma really is quite bitter,
But at least she's curbed that twitter.

September 3
Who's Steve Bannon anyway?
Who cares what he has to say,
Clinging futilely to power
When he's really past his hour?

September 4

Stephen Bannon! What a laugh!
Who would want the autograph
Of a white supremacist?
Better he should just be hissed.

September 5

Trump was hot on opioids.
Now they're something he avoids.
That concern is long since gone.
Now, as always, he moves on.

September 6

They say Trump was so choleric
Trying to clear bad son Eric.
They say he was wrong and quite daft
When he wrote that fatal first draft.

September 7

Watch out for our plump prez
And all the things he sez.
Higgly-piggly
He sez "bigly"
And calling things "so sad"
With his thick belly pad.

September 8

Why is Donald out there fixin'
To compare himself to Nixon?
Is his oddball Comey reach meant
To prepare him for impeachment?

September 9

Build the wall, yes, build the wall,
But it won't get built at all.
Trump won't disabuse his base.
He'll just laugh right in their face.

September 10

Chuck and Nancy, Chuck and Nancy.
Now Trump thinks they're very fancy.
Nancy and Chuck, Nancy and Chuck.
Now Trump thinks they'll bring him luck.

September 11

Brit PM Theresa May
Disliked what Trump had to say
Of the bomb when butting in.
Poor, dumb Donald just can't win.

September 12

Has 'Vanka vanished,
Jared been banished?
Have fam'ly and in-laws
Ignored discipline laws—
Mocked, sans chagrin, laws?

September 13

No one has descended faster
Than the great H. R. McMaster.
Truth is, there's no one who could win
Giving Trump's canards a good spin.

September 14

Trump visited the UN—
Prob'ly won't be asked again—
Calling Kim the Rocket Man.
Let's call Trump the Block It Man.
Let's call him the Mock It Man.
Let's call him the Shock It Man.
Let's call him the Crock "It" Man.
Let's call him the Schlock "It" Man.

September 15

As for that repeal bill
Set forth with no honest skill
But with plenty of ill will,
Expect that it amounts to nil.

September 16

Anything Obama did
Trump believes he must get rid
Of, but he's not in the right.
He's just acting out of spite.

September 17

John McCain has had his say.
Once again, he'll get his way.
Donald Trump's still acting queer, o-
Mitting John McCain as hero.

September 18

Trump says Russia's one big hoax,
But it's not one of his jokes.
He knows that he tells a lie,
One he knows his base will buy.

September 19
Kim calls Trump a "dotard,"
But we know he's no Bard.
Let him play that low card.
Since Trump is a blowhard.

September 20
Donald Trump misunderstands
The US Constitution.
He just treats it underhand.
That's his contribution.
Wanna take a bet on him
Not knowing flag-burning's legal
And not just done on a whim?
That's our great bald eagle.

September 21
Jared abused his private email.
Lock him up, lock him up.
Ivanka abused her private email.
Lock her up, lock her up.
Bannon abused his private email.

Lock him up, lock him up.
Priebus abused his private email.
Lock him up, lock him up.
Aren't they a gang of fools,
Certain they can flout the rules?
They're outrageous as can be.
Lock them up and lose the key.

September 22

Ev'ry time Trump says, "Believe me,"
Let's respond, "You can't deceive me."
Ev'ry time he spouts the phrase,
Let's respond with lots of nays.

September 23

Hey, Tom Price,
It's not nice
Riding planes
At such high, er, price.

September 24
First Facebook,
Then Twitter
Gave space. Look,
We're bitter.

September 25
When called to account,
He decides to fight.
Criticisms mount—
He decides to bite.
When put to the test,
Isn't he the best?!

September 26
Donald Trump has had his say—
Diplomacy is not the way.
This is how he puts his checks
On Tillerson, belittled Rex.

September 27
Donald Trump gave his regards
On each fallen Vegas soul.
But how will he play his cards
When it comes to gun control?

September 28
Donald Trump, the constant freak: Oh—
Look at him in Puerto Rico,
Saying how they whacked his budget.
Always count on him to sludge it.

September 29
"It isn't his nature to help,"
A wise Virgin Islands man said.
It is in Trump's nature to yelp
When he's criticized and turns red.
This president's only a whelp
Without a true thought in his head.

September 30
Tillerson called Trump a "moron,"
Causing many more to pour on
Epithets like "unschooled," "nasty,"
"Evil," "ignorant," "bombast-y."
Any one you think to try
Is one that surely will apply.

October 2017

October 1

"The calm before the storm,"
He says, and then he winks.
He's running true to form:
He simply never thinks.

October 2

Will Mattis and will Kelly act
With Tillerson upon their pact?
The three vowed they would suicide
If Trump no more they could abide.
Now does it seem they'll follow through?
So many hope they will. Do you?

October 3

49ers take a knee.
VP Pence and family
Head off to the nearest gate,
Acting on Trump's rule of hate.

October 4

Don't you love the great Bob Corker?
He is just, well, one true corker,
Scoring on the White House lad,
Who will never say, "My bad."

October 5

Trump boasts of his high IQ.
Trump is not at all like you.
High Ignorance Quotient is his aim.
Aren't you glad you're not the same?

October 6

Frankly, it is not much fun
Watching Trump become undone.
Daily getting worse, now he
Is attacking NBC.

October 7

Long as Trump can boast his wealth
He cares zip about your health.
Take Obama's healthcare bill:
He is out to gut it still.

October 8

Why does Trump attack Iran?
He does that because he can.
He says he dislikes their spirit.
He'll do all he can to queer it.

October 9

Trump said he would drain the swamp,
But he's having one big romp.
Do the folks who form his base
Know the swamp is now stuffed space?

October 10

Living in the Age of Trump
Means we're living in a dump.
Harvey Weinstein's one example.
Pretty soon, more will be ample.

October 11

Donald Trump will take no blame
For the Congress lapses.
GOP folks say the same
Of his bum synapses.

October 12

Trump declares he "won't be pretty."
We all know he can't be witty.
Normally, he's only…well…
Perhaps the poor schlub needs our pity.

October 13

Ring! Ring! Trump is calling.
Why should we be grateful?
Better, let's start stalling.
He'll say something hateful.
Ring! Ring! Trump is ringing.
Oh, no! Let's start cringing.
Is there news he's bringing?
No, he's just unhinging.
Ring! Ring! Trump is phoning.
He'll call someone "wacky"!
He'll get us to moaning.
He is always tacky.

October 14

I sat down to watch the telly.
That's when I observed John Kelly.
He was criticizing gratis
Rep. F. Wilson. Poof! His status.

October 15

McCain, Corker, Flake—
How much will they take?
They will take no more
Trump, whom they deplore.

October 16

What about that Breitbart Steve,
Our premier supremacist?
Focus he will not receive
Once we cross him off our list.

October 17

John McCain talks of rich bone spurs.
Donald Trump brings up his own spurs.
Which one would you call a hero?
Which one would you dub a zero?

October 18

Trump's mem'ry is the very best.
The man is all superlatives.
In fact, those rank superlatives
Are all that Donald ever gives.

October 19
Twitter's dropped the Russian bots.
There were lots and lots and lots.
Now if Twitter would just dump
All the lying tweets from Trump.

October 20
Here's some Saturday excitement:
Mueller has a sealed indictment.
How will this affect Trump's views
That this all is just fake news?

October 21
Jared doings?
Fewer viewings.
'Vanka also.
Newsy calls? No.

October 22
"No, no, no, it's Hillary,"
The White House liar pleas.
"She's the one to pillory
And not my travesties."

October 23

That George Papadopoulos—
What a big surprise for us.
Now the White House chief inquires,
"Who here might be wearing wires?"

October 24

Any time that Trump is acting,
He is working at distracting.
He believes that his deflecting
Keeps us all from our suspecting
What he's up to is suspicious—
Something stupid, something vicious.

October 25

Of the New York truck attacks,
He unleashed some new fake facts
Blaming Schumer, many more—
Donald Trump, the world-class bore.

October 26

AG Sessions lies
And John Kelly lies.
Jared Kushner lies.
All those lying guys—
Each gross liar vies
For Trump's Liar Prize.

October 27

Here's a boast that Donald chatters:
"I'm the only one that matters."
Here's one more to which he sticks. It—
'S "I'm the only one to fix it."
He sure likes himself a lot.
Too bad most of us do not.

October 28

Off Trump goes for twelve full days,
Hoping he reaps foreign praise.
But we all know he's ill-equipped—
Only sometimes sticks to script.

October 29

Commerce sec'y Wilbur Ross
Doesn't like to take a loss.
So he's held to one, at least,
Income booster that's increased.

October 30

Mental illness is the cause,
Trump declared without a pause.
That expression truly stuns.
Metal illness kills with guns.

October 31

Who's next?
Perplexed?
Great fun—
Flynn, son.

November 2017

November 1
Murphy, Northam hit the stump
And defeated Donald Trump.
Let's see Sarah Sanders's spins
On these two decisive wins.

November 2
Thanks to the Brits
Who've kept their wits,
A new poll shows
Trump's global lows.

November 3
Is anyone whom Trump has tagged
Not been shamed and then been dragged
Through the swamp he swore he'd drain?
Breathes there one who's made a gain?

November 4

Trump remains convinced he can peddle
That his Putin pal wouldn't meddle
In this country's many elections.
He won't accept convincing objections.

November 5

Duterte he so admires
And of Putin never tires.
He adores the autocrats.
In his belfry he has bats.

November 6

Let's deplore
AL's Roy Moore,
Then abhor
Him some more.

November 7

Donald Jr. keeps them coming—
Revelations mighty numbing.
Bet there's plenty up his sleeve
Since he's practiced to deceive.

November 8
Donald Trump is back from China
Saying things could not be fina,
Claiming bonds have reached new heights,
Sure, he left out civil rights.

November 9
Jared Kushner's documents
Still don't make a lot of sense.
He keeps holding info back.
He shares Junior's moral lack.

November 10
Franken gets a crude Trump tweet,
Nothing for AL's Moore.
Trump emits another bleat
Rotten to the core.

November 11
Mueller's spotlight's on Hope Hicks.
Does she know how Donald ticks?
Since she's always in the room,
Will she seal Donald's doom?

November 12

Emoluments are his joy,
Our prez, the chief fat cat.
He says to the hoi polloi,
"Just get used to that!"

November 13

Trump now has a new disaster,
Courtesy of Gen. McMaster.
When the "idiot" word is used,
So-called prez is not amused.

November 14

Trump pardoned a turkey today—
An act that now prompts me to say,
"My heart hasn't hardened.
The turkey he pardoned
Was not himself. Hip hip hooray!"

November 15

"Do you think they'll get the president?"
Jared wants to know.
Do you think they'll get the president?
We all hope it's so.

November 16

Not ev'ry Trump hotel
Is doing very well.
The one in New York's Soho
Has now become a no-no.
Could it be that Trump-dot-org
Is now heading to the morgue?

November 17

Mike Flynn's lawyer?
Ex-employer?
Now not talking.
More like stalking.
Mueller's arrows—
Outcome narrows.

November 18

Trump's boasting, "Once again I'm
There on the cover of Time.
Then again maybe I'm not.
Still, I sure love me a lot."

November 19

Ivanka's dissing Moore,
The one her father's for.
Has she gone disloyal.
Is Daddy on the boil?

November 20

Trump calls her Pocahontas
At any time he can.
He thinks he's gonna taunt us,
That petty little man.

November 21

Trump keeps after CNN
Once again and then again,
Tweeting out against free speech,
Clinging on, just like a leech.

November 22

No government shutdown.
Instead, shut that nut down?
Let's muzzle that idjit,
That mad mental midget.

November 23

Our president, our head of state,
Is happiest retweeting hate.
The damage that can't be undone
Makes him someone we need to shun.

November 24

Trump is at the White House shaking.
Trump is at the White House quaking.
Trump is at the White House breaking.
Trump is at the White House faking.

November 25

There's nothing Donald Trump won't try,
Nothing of which he hangs shy.
No institute he won't defy,
Now he stalks the FBI.
What a champion! What a guy!

November 26

John Dowd scripted Donald's tweet.
It's a task he proudly claims.
But Dowd's now in full retreat.
He is going down in flames.

November 27

Hogwash! Bushwah! And pshaw!
Trump is not above the law.
But he is beneath contempt.
From that take he's not exempt.

November 28

Jerusalem has been Trump's goal.
It is "in his heart and soul."
Most folks don't know where to start.
Has he a soul? Has he a heart?

November 29

Attorney/client privilege, say what?
Donald Trump Jr., that well-known nut,
Thinks he has found his new dodge, his out,
Proving he's guilty, and there is no doubt.

November 30

So what if Trump attended schools?
So did a lot of other fools.
The claim that he is educated
Is grossly exaggerated.

December 2017

December 1

Trump says, "The system's rigged."
So once again he's pigged.
That's now his sad, sad song
Whenever he is wrong.

December 2

White House paranoia
We all can now enjoy. Ya
Know that Trump is paranoid
About the truths he won't avoid.

December 3

A stunning new statistic
To make you go ballistic:
D. Trump lies five times daily,
Which makes him kinda jail-y.

December 4

Hooray for Doug Jones.
He'll rattle Trump's bones.
His winning event
Begins Trump's descent.

December 5

Donald will be mighty cross
If he's blamed for Roy Moore's loss.
He knew from the get-go
Moore'd reap that 'Bama let-go.

December 6

When Trump gets his daily brief,
He gives back all kinds of grief.
He scorns any facts, you bet.
They just get him so upset.

December 7

Trump dislikes the FBI,
And he slams the DOJ.
There is nothing he won't try,
Nothing crude that he won't say.

December 8

Have you ever stopped to ponder
Just how wrong a mind can wander?
Examples of this state are many,
Donald Trump's the worst of any.

December 9

Dear oh, dear oh, dear oh!
Fox's Jeanine Pirro
Visited the White House,
Where they said with spite, "Raus!"
Her attacks on Mueller
Packed too much wrong color.

December 10

Trump lists what he's achieved
Throughout his long first year.
The bull that he has heaved
Is surely without peer.

December 11

Trump now has his will.
Trump now has his bill.
But let's wait until
All has come to nil.

December 12

Watch those spineless GOPs
Praising Don down on their knees,
Begging their Narcissus Trump,
"May I kiss you on the rump?"—
Saying to him, "Tell you what,
Let me plant one on your butt."
Saying something just like this:
"On your butt I'll plant a kiss.
You're the ultimate in crass.
Please, please, let me kiss your ass."

December 13

Trump, committed bully,
Always at it fully,
With those gifts unfurled,
He bullies the world.

December 14

Is there a Trump-like ban on
The terrible Steve Bannon,
The one once thought so bright, smart
And now sent back to Breitbart?
He predicts Trump's one term.
He loves making Trump squirm.

December 15

GOP—the new career
Is that they're all out to smear
Mueller and the FBI.
There's no trick they will not try,
They are all so damned afraid
Trump is likely to be stayed
That they play their dark charade.

December 16

"You're all richer," Trump told friends
Down at Mar-a-Lago.
So that's how the tax bill trends,
How events in Fla. go.

December 17
Donald Trump again
Stomps on CNN.
Freedom of the press?
He fights for much less.

December 18
A friend of Bill O'Reilly,
Who knew him back at school:
"Trump's pal was never wily.
He only was a tool."

December 19
Would you call a color bad?
Red or blue, would you term sad?
No, you wouldn't. All the same,
Trump gives orange a bad name.

December 20
Mike Huckabee says
That our current prez
Is like Winston Churchill.
Well, don't that besmirch all?!

December 21
One thing Trump is not controlling
Is the ever-constant polling.
Any way he tries to boil it,
He still ends up in the toilet.

December 22
"Collusion is a hoax"—
That's not one of Trump's jokes.
But here's a little clue:
He knows collusion's true.

December 23
"When he does it, he's shirking.
When I do it, I'm working."
What's Trump talking about?
"Golf," he says through his pout.

December 24
Papadopoulos,
Whom we now discuss,
Was a coffee boy
With more to deploy.

December 25
Trump dislikes those regulations.
He sees them as aggravations.
If Obama stood behind them,
He makes sure he's undermined them.

December 26

You got a button?
Your button's nuttin'.
You got a charger?
My charger's larger.
You got a fire?
My flames are higher.
You got a glider?
My glider's wider.
You got a trawler?
My trawler's taller.
You got a freighter?
My freighter's greater.
You got a goosie?
My goose is looser.
You got a penis?
Mine reaches Venus.
I'm rubber, you're glue.
Whatever you say bounces off me and sticks to you.

December 27

Everybody, take a look!
Michael Wolff's revealing book
Goes behind the White House walls
To expose the daily mauls,
Proving that the wretched place
Is a national disgrace.

December 28

Trumps moans a moan:
"Where's my Roy Cohn?"
Best ask instead,
"Where is my head?"

December 29

Does he snit,
Throw a fit?
Is he Mitt
Or nitwit?
Should he quit?
Should he git?
Should he split?
Sure as spit.

December 30

Smart?! Smart?! Trump's not merely smart.
That is only the very basic start.
Genius! Genius! That's what our Trump is!
The world's outstanding, foremost mental whiz!

December 31

Bannon's backing down—
That infernal clown.
Bannon's pushing back—
That pathetic hack.
Here comes crawling Steve
Begging for reprieve.

January 2018

January 1

The sun rose again today brighter than it has ever been,
Thanks to Donald Trump.
Water has been wetter this past year than it's ever been,
Thanks to Donald Trump.
Blue skies not only nationally but also internationally
  are bluer than ever before,
Thanks to Donald Trump.
Planes are landing far more safely than ever in recorded
  history,
Thanks to Donald Trump.
20/20 vision is now more 20/20 than at any time since
  optometry was refined,
Thanks to Donald Trump.
The list just goes on and on,
Thanks to Donald Trump.
Indeed, lists themselves are now longer, more comprehensive
  and meaningful,
Thanks to Donald Trump.
Thank you, thank you, thank you, Donald Trump.

January 2

Something Trump declares one day
Tuesday isn't what he'll say.
Wednesday he will change his mind.
Thursday he'll have redefined.

January 3

Trump wants to change the libel laws,
Insisting that they're full of flaws.
But when it comes to spreading lies,
It's Trump himself who takes the prize.

January 4

Donald Trump celebrates:
"Dig it!
I'm a bigot!"

January 5

Trump speaks:
"What is FISA? I don't know.
Fill me in and make it slow.
I know nothing much, it's true,
But I'll act as if I do."

January 6

Here's a nationwide adventure:
Getting Trump a needed censure.
Do it now and make it fast, too,
'Cause it's definitely past due.

January 7

"I'm not a racist,"
Trump insists.
Still, he's the basest
On all lists.

January 8

Trump said that he'd be boring.
He promised that he would.
He said he'd have us snoring.
Oh, if he only could.

January 9

Trump never hits a norm.
He just reverts to form.
Beneath the orange frizz
He's always who he is.

January 10

Trump made a great big payoff
So Stormy D. would stray off,
The media would lay off.
He never takes a day off.

January 11

Does Trump want a shutdown
As a chance to putt down
Or just set his butt down?
Best he cuts his gut down.

January 12

Donald's tweets are never petty.
They are also far from witty.
He'll just lie and lie and lie—
Fake news for his base to buy.

January 13

"An incredibly successful first year,"
That dear Sarah Sanders will cheer,
Which once again proves that it's true
She's fully delusional, too.

January 14

Melania, that silent soul,
Practices great self-control,
Or does her so calm composure
Mean she's signed a non-disclosure?

January 15

Trump will make ev'ry attempt—
While, as usual, he's unkempt—
To distract and to preempt.
The Yiddish word for him? Verklempt.

January 16

If you believe
That he's naïve,
Then you're a tool
For that big fool.
The guy was shown
Schemes by Roy Cohn.

January 17

Donald Trump is now six-three,
Taller than he used to be,
And the prezzie's height increase
Explains why he's not obese.

January 18

Michael Cohen's LLC
Paid out Stormy's hefty fee.
Cohen said, "Oh, what the hell,
I'll create a handy shell."

January 19

Is this now McConnell's shutdown,
Or is it a Chuck Schumer shutdown?
Better yet a Don Trump shutdown?
What is it? What kinda what-down?

January 20

Humpty Trumpty hit a brick wall.
Humpty Trumpty's fated to fall,
But all US sources and all US men
May never put America back together again.

Made in the USA
Middletown, DE
24 September 2020